# 101 QUESTIONS & ANSWERS

## ABOUT CLASSICAL MUSIC

DARREN HENLEY & TIM LIHOREAU

BOOSEY & HAWKES

Boosey & Hawkes Music Publishers Ltd
www.boosey.com

*Also available from Boosey & Hawkes, by the same authors:*

| | |
|---|---|
| The Classic FM Pocket Book of Music | 978-0-85162-430-3 |
| The Classic FM Pocket Book of Quotes | 978-0-85162-451-8 |
| The Classic FM Pocket Book of Trivia | 978-0-85162-449-5 |
| Classic Ephemera | 978-0-85162-467-9 |

Published by Boosey & Hawkes Music Publishers Ltd,
in association with Classic FM



ISBN 978-0-85162-450-1

First impression 2008

Cover design by Design United
Printed in England by The Halstan Print Group, Amersham, Bucks

**www.boosey.com**
**www.classicfm.com**

# Introduction

This little book is a by-product of more than 15 years of making programmes at Classic FM, the world's biggest classical music radio station. The next hundred or so pages contain the answers to 101 questions that we have either been asked the most often, that we have enjoyed answering the most, or that we wish someone had asked.

If there is a question you want answered in future editions, then please do contact us online at: **www.classicfm.com/101QandA**

*Darren Henley*
*Tim Lihoreau*

## 1: What is classical music?

Our very first question and we have two answers for you. If you are overly mathematically inclined, please count these as two halves of the same answer – otherwise we've shot our book's title to pieces before we've really got started. Firstly, "classical music" is a period of music from around 1730 to 1820, in which Haydn, Mozart and Beethoven were all composing. It takes its name from the "classicism" which inspired people around this time and saw the major development of the symphony.

Secondly, "classical music" is also a label for all music in the Western acoustic tradition, often using the instruments of the orchestra and featuring a system of notation developed over centuries. So, the orchestral music of Frederick Delius and the organ music of J S Bach, while not classical under the terms of our first definition, are, nevertheless "classical music".

## 2: Who invented musical notes?

A man called Guido, from Arezzo in Italy. He was a Benedictine monk, famous in his lifetime not just for his work on the theory of music, but also because he was reputed to be able to train singers to learn songs in super-fast time. His most notable tome is *Micrologus,* which contains his own unique system for writing music down, originally called the "Guidonian" method. It's still around today, more or less, give or take the odd tweak.

## 3: Who killed Mozart?

As exciting as it might be to believe that the composer Salieri had Mozart bumped off from some sort of Viennese grassy knoll, it now seems most likely that Mozart simply fell victim to kidney disease, possibly brought on by having eaten some under-cooked pork chops. Mozart may have put it about that his *Requiem* was commissioned by the devil himself, but it was actually a local nobleman who was responsible. Scholars also dispute his own deathbed claims that he was poisoned.

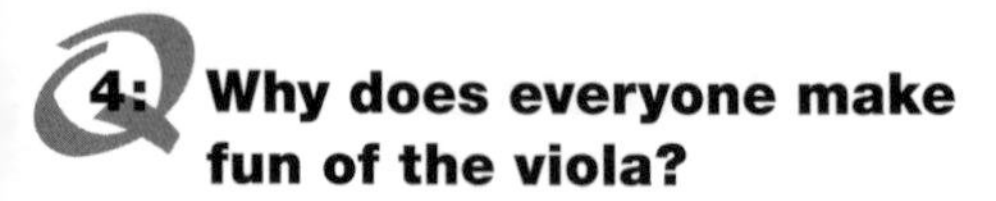

## 4: Why does everyone make fun of the viola?

Well, they certainly do in orchestral circles. The viola's register is designed for playing in the middle. Not up high, where it might get all the striking lead lines, nor down low where it might at least get the menacing *Jaws* tunes. Hence, it is sometimes seen as, dare we say, a bit dull.

By the way: what's the difference between a viola and a trampoline? You take your shoes off when you jump up and down on a trampoline.

## 5: Is film music proper classical music?

The snobs say not. We say a resounding "yes". Writing film music is as worthy as stumping up your latest symphony. Indeed, we reckon that, were some of history's greatest composers around today, they would be lapping up the big commissions. There's a big case to be argued that the likes of John Williams have done more for the cause of classical music in the 20th and 21st centuries than all the squeaky gate★ merchants put together.

---

★ See question 60

## 6: What is the "Enigma" in the *Enigma Variations*?

There isn't just one enigma surrounding Elgar's *Variations on an Original Theme,* commonly known as *The Enigma Variations.* There are at least two mysteries and maybe even three. The first enigma is that of the names of the individuals represented in each movement of the work. Elgar chose to paint a musical picture of a number of his friends while keeping their identity secret. In the years since, this code has been broken, with movements centring on his publisher, his wife Alice and even the composer himself. More enigmatic altogether is his claim that there is a hidden theme, secreted in or around the work. Even *more* enigmatic is the idea that the word "theme" might not even mean "tune" in this instance, but something altogether more ethereal. Boffins the world over have spent years trying to come up with theories of what the theme might have been – from *God Save the Queen* to *I've Got a Lovely Bunch of Coconuts.*★ Like all good enigmas, Elgar took the secret with him to the grave.

---

★ Highly unlikely

## Is the Cor Anglais actually English?

Simple answer to this one: no. It's most likely to have originated in Western Poland. This instrument is, in fact, just an oboe, but one with an end section modified to be bulb-shaped and sounding a little lower in pitch than the oboe. When it was first heard, the sound was thought to resemble angels, so it was given the German word "engellisch", meaning angelic. The thing is ... "engellisch" also meant English. And "English Horn" is the phrase that stuck.

# 8: Who was William Tell?

Rossini's hero probably didn't exist at all. His legend comes from a period when Austria was trying to dominate Switzerland. An Austrian dignitary put his hat on a pole and insisted locals bowed to it. William Tell refused and, as punishment, he was ordered to shoot an apple from his son's head with his crossbow. He told his Austrian tormentor that had he missed, he would have fired a second bolt at him. The defiance inspired the Swiss to rebel and form their own confederation.

## 9: How long can a piece of classical music last?

There are no hard and fast rules. John Cage has written a work called *Organ2/ ASLSP* (the *ASLSP* takes its letters from *As Slow aS Possible*). The piece is usually played to last around twenty minutes, but, of course, with a direction to play "as slow as possible", then anything is possible. A current performance started in September 2001 and is due to end in September 2640. That's exactly 639 years later. Incidentally, don't miss the next exciting change of chord in *Organ2/ ASLSP* on 5 July 2012. The best bit of this whole barmy story though is that, as this performance is taking place in a church – a real, living, working church – they have built a transparent, acrylic cube around the organ pipes, so that you can't hear it! So the man who brought us *4′33″* of silence is having a last laugh that lasts for 639 years!

## 10: Why is Haydn known as "Papa"?

Let's rule out the spurious answers. It's not short for Papageno. He wasn't Pope. And he wasn't the boss of the Smurfs. He *was* a towering figure in the classical music scene and his influence stretched far and wide over many who came after him. He counselled, nurtured and advised. Separately, he was also known as "the father of the symphony", reflecting how much he had developed this particular genre in his own work.

## 11: Who was the most prolific composer?

*The Guinness Book of World Records* awards this title to Telemann, on the basis of the number of works he left behind. It seems he composed music at much the same rate as us mere mortals breathe. By the end of his life he was well on the way to having written a total of 3,700 separate compositions. But here's the rub. Some of them only last for a minute or two.

## 12: What is minimalist music?

Whereas a minimalist house might have pure white walls and no clutter, a minimalist piece of music uses repeated patterns of notes, over and over again. Sometimes, this endless repetition can seem frenetic and busy, while at other times it can be used to sow the seeds of hypnotic tranquillity. Philip Glass's *Violin Concerto* is a good example of the latter type. For many, minimalist music is like an olive – very much an acquired taste. For others, it can become a life's passion. Check out another minimalist composer: Steve Reich.

## 13: Why is Mozart's *Piano Concerto No 21* known as 'Elvira Madigan'?

Simply because it was used in the 1967 film *Elvira Madigan.* It was an obscure, Swedish love story, which, as far as we know, is the only one whose heroine is a rope-walker. It was nominated for a Bafta and a Golden Globe and its wonderful cinematography was enhanced by the soundtrack. Vivaldi's *Violin Concerto in E* was also used in the film, but it has never been given the *Elvira Madigan* label.

## 14: Do composers always come up with their own original tunes?

You might think that the answer would be a simple "yes". Sometimes, though, it's a resounding "no". Often composers use other people's musical themes and write their own variations to them. Examples of this include *Rhapsody on a Theme of Paganini* by Rachmaninoff and *A Young Person's Guide to the Orchestra* in which Britten borrowed a theme composed by Purcell. And then there's Bizet. He didn't actually write the *Habanera* in his opera *Carmen.* Instead, he adapted it from a song called *El arreglito* by a Spanish composer called Iradier.

Baroque composers often pinched tunes that they had heard and passed them off as their own. With our modern communications networks, this would be a far harder trick to pull off today. One composer, Tomaso Albinoni even had a Doppelgänger, who passed himself off as the real thing for years. Albinoni only discovered the fraudster's existence when a fan wrote to him complimenting him on a concert in Munich that he had never given.

## 15: Why do hymn tunes have names that are different from their lyrics?

Every hymn has a name for its tune and it keeps this name, even if somebody sets new words to it. So, for example, the standard tune for *The Lord's My Shepherd* is known as *Crimond*, because the composer, Jessie Irvine, was living in the Scottish village of Crimond when she wrote it. The words to *The Lord's My Shepherd* can be sung to several other tunes though, such as *Belmont*, *Evan*, *Orlington* or *Wiltshire*.

## 16: Who were the Pearl Fishers from the duet?

Their names are Zurga and, somewhat unfortunately, Nadir. In 'Au fond du temple saint', they are both reminiscing about the beautiful girl they once saw, called Leila, whom they both agreed not to pursue, instead declaring undying friendship for each other. This opera isn't staged very often, which might have something to do with the need for an enormous funeral pyre on stage at the end. Health and Safety would probably have something to say about it.

## 17: How many instruments make up an orchestra?

Again, two answers. Answer A: around 85 to 100. Answer B: around 15 to 20.

How so? Well, in terms of numbers, around 85 to 100 players make up a modern normal-sized symphony orchestra.

In terms of different instruments, though, because there are banks and banks of some and just one or two of others, the actual number of different instruments is between 15 and 20. It breaks down as follows: violins (around 34 of them), violas (12 or so), cellos (10), double basses (8),

harp (1), flute (3), piccolo (1), clarinet (3), bassoon (3), double bassoon (1), horn (6), trumpet (4), trombone (4), tuba (1), timpani (1), percussion (2), piano (1) and so on.
So, somewhere around 100 players and 20 different instruments.

## 18: Did Mozart and Beethoven ever meet?

They did, when Beethoven was just a sixteen-year-old boy. The young Ludwig travelled to Vienna to play for Mozart. The older man agreed to give him lessons, but suddenly Beethoven was summoned home because his mother was gravely ill. By the time he visited Vienna again, some five and a half years later, Mozart was dead.

## 19: When was the last castrato still singing?

The height of the world's obsession with castrati was the middle 1700s, when possibly the most famous, known as Farinelli (although his real name was Carlo Broschi), plied his trade. The man with the dubious honour of being "the last castrato" was Alessandro Moreschi, who died in 1921. Despite the Pope banning castrati from the Papal Chapel in 1903, Moreschi was certainly still singing elsewhere as late as 1914. Uniquely, he left behind a series of early gramophone recordings of his voice.

## 20: What is the order of singing voices?

From the top down, here goes. Ladies first: sopranos, mezzo-sopranos, altos. And then the fellows: countertenor (the male version of alto), tenor, baritone, bass-baritone, bass. Above the women is the treble, usually a boy's voice, but occasionally a girl's.

## 21: What are opus numbers?

*Opus* is the Latin word for "work". An opus number is attached to each work that a composer has written to differentiate it from all of the others. Giving each work a unique catalogue number is not only useful, it's sometimes essential. Composers often write several works with the same name. Take Chopin, for example. He composed 50 pieces all called *Muzurka*, so the opus numbers come in more than handy.

## 22: Why don't all composers' works have opus numbers?

These usually originate from the somewhat obsessive individuals who have taken it upon themselves to catalogue composers' entire outputs. Mozart's man, Mr Köchel, is probably the most famous, leaving behind K numbers. Lucky old Scarlatti had two cataloguers, Mr Kirkpatrick (another set of K numbers), and Mr Longo (L numbers). As you'd expect in classical music, nothing is ever as simple as it might be. So, naturally, these two sets of numbers don't actually match.

## 23: What does Baroque mean?

If we said “a pearl of irregular or bulbous shape”, you’d probably think we’d gone mad. Only that *is* what it originally meant. It comes from the Portuguese word “barroco”, which was applied to jewellery and only transferred across to music and the arts in the 1730s. It now applies to the entire period of music from around 1600 to 1750.

## 24: What should one wear to a classical concert?

Whatever makes you feel comfortable. We think the days where attendance at a classical music concert necessitated a trip to Savile Row are over. Jeans mingle with suits and Gap sits alongside Gucci. Even the orchestras aren't always suited and booted these days, with many taking a leaf out of the Kiwi Rugby team's handbook by favouring all black. For soloists, of course, it's more a case of "Go on ... I dare you!" There really are no rules.

## 25: What is it about opera and murder?

Murders are an integral part of many operas. One of the bloodiest is *Lulu* by the 20th-century composer Alban Berg. There's a death by heart attack and a suicide in Act 1, a murder committed by the heroine in Act 2 and another one in Act 3. Then, the heroine and a friend are themselves murdered by none other than Jack the Ripper.

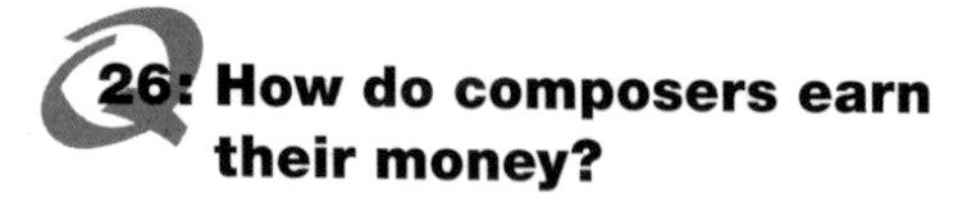

## 26: How do composers earn their money?

There is an old joke which goes: why don't composers look out of the window in the morning? Because it would give them nothing to do in the afternoon. Yes, a composer's life can be tough. A recent report estimated that there are fewer than a thousand people in the UK who earn a full-time living from composing – and that is including television and film composers, as well as those working in the rock and pop worlds. Classical composers are often "day jobbers", who squeeze composing time out of a candle that has burnt down to the middle from both ends.

In Mozart's time, a composer would earn most from his commissions – that is the original payment to produce the piece. Nowadays, though, composers increasingly make their money from the royalties which come afterwards, whether for publishing, performance or recording and playback.

## 27: What was *Susannah's* Secret?

It's the name of an opera by Ermanno Wolf-Ferrari. The plot centres on a Count, who thinks his wife, Susannah, has a secret lover because he has smelt tobacco around the house. One day he catches her outside puffing away on a fag, when she should be in the drawing room. It turns out that Susannah's secret is that she smokes. When the count discovers his mistake, he vows to take up the habit too. Smoking bans had not been invented back then.

## 28: Why did everyone hate Wagner?

In short, he wasn't a very nice bloke. Take this quote as an example: "I am not like other people ... the world owes me what I need. I can't live on a miserable organist's pittance, like your master, Bach!" He was a thoroughly unpleasant, racist, megalomaniac egocentric and a serial philanderer to boot. He repeatedly bit the hand that fed him, bankrupting the opera house that commissioned him. His music is, on the other hand, absolutely fantastic stuff.

## 29: Of whom were the Impressionist composers doing an impression?

They certainly weren't the Rory Bremners of their day. In painting, impressionism began with Monet's *Impression, Sunrise* and continued right up to Pissarro and Cézanne, via Sisley, Renoir and even Turner. In music, it was very much a French thing, with the works of Debussy and Ravel figuring highly, containing *aural* pictures, or impressions.

## 30: Which is the world's oldest orchestra?

Founded in 1548, when Mary Queen of Scots was just five years old, the Dresden Staatskapelle Orchestra is generally reckoned to be the oldest orchestra still going. One of its earliest guiding lights was the composer Heinrich Schütz. In the years since, it has gone on to be associated with some of the greatest conductors in history. Fritz Reiner, Karl Böhm and Bernard Haitink all did stints with the baton at the Staatskapelle.

## 31: What's the difference between a 'Symphony Orchestra' and a 'Philharmonic Orchestra'?

The word "philharmonic" simply means "music-loving". So when groups of music-loving folk got together, they often called themselves "philharmonic societies". Symphony, which means "playing together", and Philharmonic are the orchestral equivalent of the addition "United" or "Rovers" in football. Either will do, it's just down to the personal choice of the people who founded them.

## 32: Where is the 'Paradise Garden'?

In Delius's opera *A Village Romeo and Juliet*, the Paradise Garden is not an idyllic heavenly vale. Instead, it is the local village pub. The opera's hero and heroine, Sali and Vreli, are prevented from marrying because their families are enemies. One night they walk to the local pub, dance to a fiddler's tunes and then die in a lovers' suicide pact. You might need a drink yourself after all that.

## 33: How did Gregorian Chant get its name?

Let's split it up. "Chant" is short for plainchant, often called plainsong, which is a one-line, unaccompanied tune, very often not sung in any strict metre, but sung in order to match its words. Pope Gregory the First generally gets the credit for sorting out and writing down the whole "plainchant" business, even if his role might have been slightly overstated. He certainly leant his name to this type of chant.

## 34: How did the saxophone get its name?

There was no Mr Trump responsible for the trumpet and no Mr Trombo who created the trombone. But there was an Adolphe Sax, who was born in 1814. He filed umpteen records at the French patent office for his musical instrument inventions, including saxhorns, saxotrombas and even "rational bassoons" (don't ask – life's too short). His saxophone is his greatest legacy, for which, sadly, he was only granted a fifteen-year patent.

## 35: Why did Wagner write such long operas?

Wagner, was, shall we say, an extremely confident man. That's diplomatic speak for "complete megalomaniac". So, if he felt like writing pages of music, he jolly well was *going* to write pages of music. He was writing towards the end of the Romantic period of classical music, when bigger was better. He was also lucky enough to be bankrolled by an indulgent royal patron and so money was no object. That meant he could go on writing … and writing … and writing …

## 36: What does the Master of the Queen's Music do?

This is the musical equivalent of the Poet Laureate. The honour is awarded to a composer of great distinction, currently Sir Peter Maxwell Davies. The job comes with a small stipend and an expectation to compose music for royal occasions or commemorations. The role has its origins in the middle ages, when "the Musick" was the name given to the band of musicians and minstrels employed to play for the monarch.

## 37: What is the Chapel Royal?

Let's clear up a common misconception first. The Chapel Royal is not a building. Originally, it was the name given to the body of priests and singers formed to serve the spiritual needs of the sovereign. They used to travel with the King or Queen wherever they went – even onto battlefields such as Agincourt. Today, their home is in the chapel of St James's Palace.

## 38: What was the first opera?

It is generally reckoned that *Dafne* by Jacopo Peri is the world's first ever opera, written for the Florence Carnival in 1597–8. He then wrote *Euridice* for a large Medici wedding in 1600. History has looked kindlier on Monteverdi's opera *L'Orfeo,* which was first performed in Venice in 1607. As a result, while Peri may have actually written the first ever opera, Monteverdi often claims the crown, as the composer of the first ever opera that is still in the repertoire today.

## 39: Which composer's music is played most often on Classic FM?

A multiple choice question from us for you: is it Mozart, Beethoven, Arnold, or none of the above. If you plumped for Arnold, then you would be correct, but it's not the British composer Sir Malcolm Arnold. Instead, Classic FM's most played composer is David Arnold. He wrote the Classic FM jingle, which was first heard at the station's inception at 6am on 7 September 1992 – and has been played virtually every hour since, now in its new, modernised, pared-down form.

## 40: Who was *Zadok the Priest*?

Zadok was an Israelite high priest, who lived in the 10th century BC. In the Bible, Zadok was told by David to go, along with the prophet Nathan, to anoint Solomon king over all Israel and to blow a trumpet and say, “God save King Solomon”. Handel set this biblical text to music in 1727 for the coronation of King George II. The work has been played at British coronations ever since.

## 41: Just how many different Bachs actually were there?

This is the musical dynasty to end all musical dynasties. *The New Grove Dictionary of Music and Musicians,* the single most authoritative source of information on classical music, lists no fewer than 79 people over various generations, who were organists, composers and musicians. These days, only four are much remembered outside the cemetery gates. The big one is Johann Sebastian. Then there are his three sons, Carl Philipp Emanuel, Johann Christian and Johann Christoph Friedrich.

## 42: Why was Johann Sebastian Bach fascinated with the number 14?

It's all to do with his name. He took each of the letters B-A-C-H and gave them a numerical value depending on where they came in the alphabet and then he added them all together. For the less numerically aware, the sum looks like this: 2+1+3+8=14. He was interested in mathematics and used the number to create numerical patterns of notes in his music.

## 43: When do you clap at a concert?

It is the norm to wait until the end of a complete work. So, if you're listening to a symphony – usually in four sections – you clap after the fourth movement. If it's a concerto, you tend to wait for all three movements to finish before bursting into applause. Sometimes, it's best to buy a programme and check because occasionally two movements might run into one, or the work might have been written in an unorthodox number of sections. An alternative answer is to clap whenever you want to within reason, so long as nobody is actually playing on stage. A standing ovation complete with Mexican Wave in the middle of the slow movement of the Grieg *Piano Concerto* might impair the mood a tad. Certainly, at the time much of classical music was *originally* written, concert-going was a very unstuffy experience, with audiences applauding throughout the performance. If in doubt, our advice is to stay quiet until the moment when the rest of the auditorium erupts in appreciation.

## 44: Why do opera singers warble?

It's called *vibrato* and, to varying degrees, most opera singers do it. They eventually develop a *natural* vibrato, often considered more attractive than a pure voice, such as that of a boy treble. In Baroque times, it's thought that vibrato was not nearly so pronounced in singers as it became later on, in the Romantic period. String players also have a standard vibrato, which they produce by shaking the finger that presses down the string on their instrument.

## 45: Why do most CDs seem to last for a maximum of 74 minutes?

The compact disc was jointly developed by Phillips and Sony and the 74-minute playing time is said to have come from a desire to be able to put the whole of Beethoven's *Symphony No 9* onto one single disc. Some trivia for you now. The first classical CD released in 1982 was Claudio Arrau playing Chopin and the first pop CD was Abba's album *The Visitors.*

## 46: How do trumpet players make so many notes when there are only three buttons to press?

A trumpeter uses the combination of the three buttons (in fact, called "valves") to produce a small number of different notes, all of which are close together. Then, by varying how tight or how loose they keep their lips, they can produce the same set of notes, but either higher or lower. This is process is referred to as a trumpeter's "embouchure", a word which is actually the French term for mouthpiece.

## 47: Were Brahms and Liszt actually connected?

Brahms and Liszt *did* live around the same time – the former between 1833 and 1897, and the latter between 1811 and 1886. They definitely met up a number of times from 1853 onwards, but it appears they had rather different opinions of how music should progress. Brahms even signed his name to an article condemning Liszt's "music of the future". So, yes, they met, but no, they didn't really get on, and, as far as we know, they never got "Brahms-and-Liszt" together.

## 48: Why do orchestras always tend to wear dinner suits and dull black clothing?

To understand the formal nature of orchestral clothing, you have to look at the formal nature of the orchestra. Orchestras are expensive. When they began to develop, the only people who could actually afford to maintain them were kings, queens, dukes and what have you. If you are playing for a king, you tend to dress up. And that centuries-old tradition has stuck, with only the odd exception. These days, orchestras are becoming more informal.

## 49: What was the biggest hoax in classical music?

There are many contenders for this title, but our favourite centres on the music of modern Polish composer, Piotr Zak. His music was much appreciated by two eminent critics in the 1960s, when they heard a broadcast performance of his *Mobile for Tape and Percussion.* They appreciated it less when they were told that Mr Zak was fictional and the "music" was merely random banging of percussion instruments.

## 50: Who is the biggest-selling classical artist ever?

James Horner's soundtrack to the film *Titanic* sold in excess of 30 million copies. Andrea Bocelli's 1997 recording *Romanza* sold more than 15 million. Reports variously put Bocelli's total album sales anywhere between 20 and 50 million. But in 2002, the International Federation of the Phonographic Industry gave the late Luciano Pavarotti a platinum award in honour of his unparalleled achievements in the classical world in selling "in excess of 65 million" recordings.

## 51: What is crossover music?

"Crossover" is the term used to define the combining of any two or more types of music. In the classical world, it is generally used to apply to those artists who employ modern arrangements of classical music, or new music written in the classical style. This can often involve synthesised instruments and, occasionally, drum machines and rhythm tracks.

## 52: What happens if you take the conductor away?

If you take the conductor away from, say, a London Symphony Orchestra concert, you will almost certainly still hear a fantastic performance, particularly if they have already rehearsed the work they are playing with a conductor. If, on the other hand, you take a conductor away from a lesser orchestra's performance, then the whole thing might well fall apart. As well as beating time and cueing players, a great conductor can bring out things in the music you never knew existed.

## 53: Is it true that some people can see colours in classical music?

Yes. The composer Scriabin heard particular colours from particular musical keys. He wrote down a complete circle of correlations of the two. C was red; F# was bright blue; and E was "white with a sparkle of moonlight". The correct name for someone who joins two senses together is a synaesthesiac. Messiaen and Rimsky-Korsakov were other composers who were members of this club.

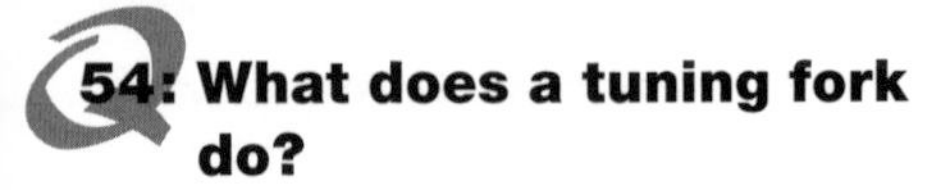

## 54: What does a tuning fork do?

This two-pronged piece of metal sounds a note very quietly when it is struck. It will always sound the same note, which is determined by the length of its prongs. Most commonly, tuning forks play the note A, as this is the note to which an orchestra tunes prior to a concert. The tuning fork was invented by a trumpeter, John Shore, who played in the premiere of many of Purcell's compositions.

## 55: Why does the oboe tune up an orchestra?

The word oboe is descended from the French "hautbois" which translates as "loud wood", and that's half the answer to this question. The oboe's penetrating sound means that it is still audible above an orchestra, even when 80-odd people are tuning and doodling around it. The other half of the answer comes from the oboe's reputation for holding its own note securely, better than any other instrument of the orchestra.

## 56: What is perfect pitch?

Perfect pitch is the ability to identify any note simply by hearing it. People with perfect pitch don't need to hear an "anchor" note first to use as a reference for any other note, they just innately know which note is which.

The authors disagree about the alternative answer to this question, with one claiming it is Elland Road, and the other, Priestfield Stadium.

## 57: Is there an exit of the Queen of Sheba?

What comes in must go out. And Handel proves the point in his oratorio, *Solomon.* The Queen sings "Illustrious Solomon, farewell", along with an air, "Will the sun forget to streak". Then Solomon says "Adieu", and they duet for a moment, before a chorus of Israelites round things off. Before you know it, the opera ends. It is at this point that the Queen of Sheba exits.

## 58: What is a Bolero?

It's a Spanish love dance, invented, so they say, by one Sebastián Cerezo, a famous Madrid hoofer from the 1780s. The word is thought to come from "volar", meaning "to fly". Cerezo was said virtually to fly around the dance floor. It's usually for two people and involves lots of dramatic bravado stamping, with arms aloft. As well as Ravel's famous *Boléro*, check out versions of the dance by Beethoven and Chopin too.

## 59: Why do people stand up during the *Hallelujah Chorus*?

When Handel's *Messiah* received its second performance, in London, King George II got to his feet when the *Hallelujah Chorus* started. As it was not the done thing to sit while the king was standing, the entire audience followed suit. Cue a tradition lasting centuries. Despite a modern tendency to insert a note in the programme asking folk to refrain, a recent internet survey suggests that the practice is certainly alive and well in the UK and the USA.

## 60: Why is some modern music so hard on the ear?

Modern classical music is not dissimilar to modern art. For some, it is an exciting "anything can happen" world. For others, it has long since lost its appeal and is merely out to shock. The composers who write this style of music (sometimes called "squeaky gate music") have a strong desire to advance their art. In the same way that Damien Hirst eschews canvas in favour of beef as a medium, so some modern composers often feel they can't still compose with simple chords and tunes.

## 61: Why are woodwind not always made of wood and brass not always made of brass?

... like the metal flute (woodwind), and the wooden alphorn (brass). The reasons are historical. Once upon a time they were. This begs the question, what would you call them instead? "Brass", for example, is far better than "the cupped-mouthpiece family". And we can't imagine young, aspiring Alison Balsoms jumping up and down shouting "Aw, mum ... I really want to be a lip-vibrating aerophone player when I grow up!" Brass and woodwind it is, then.

## 62: Was Beethoven the only major composer who was deaf?

No. Fauré went totally deaf and still continued composing. He desperately tried to cover up his failing hearing with the help of close friends. The composer of *Heart of Oak,* William Boyce, was also deaf. After the Czech composer Smetana completely lost his hearing, he wrote his *String Quartet No 1*, which included a long, high note, which he said was “the deathly whistling in my ears in the high register that, in 1874, heralded my deafness”.

## 63: Where do players in an orchestra sit?

When keyboard players were leaders of the orchestra, the rest of the players just bunched around him. Later, performers stood in a semicircle, facing the conductor or leader. Then the violins bunched to the right and left of the conductor, with the cellos and violas in the middle, the louder brass and woodwind behind. Now, all violins sit to the left, with violas and cellos to the right.

## 64: Was Holst British?

Gustavus Theodore von Holst (as he was born) may not sound the most English of names, but Holst was definitely British. His family had been in England since 1799, when his grandfather fled from St Petersburg. Holst himself was born in Cheltenham in 1874.

## 65: Why do you never see performances of Rossini's opera *Almaviva, or the Useless Precaution*?

Well, you do really. This is the alternative name for Rossini's opera *The Barber of Seville*, which was premiered in 1816. Rossini chose the title deliberately, because *Almaviva* was his version of a story which was already an opera by a composer named Paisiello, called *The Barber of Seville.* To avoid confusion (and comparisons) he went for the alternative title, but then changed it to *The Barber of Seville* at a revival in Bologna.

## 66: What do Modest Moussorgsky and Charles Aznavour have in common?

Both wrote a work called *She.* Moussorgsky's was cheerily entitled *Songs and Dances of Death* and was first published in 1882. In Russian, the word for death, *smert*, is feminine and for a long time, Moussorgsky called the work "She", perhaps a bit like the evil Voldemort being referred to as "he who must not be named" in the Harry Potter books. Just for the record, Charles Aznavour's *She* reached number one in the pop charts in 1974.

## 67: How much did Bach receive in payment for his Brandenburgs?

The *Brandenburg Concertos* were put together in 1721, when Bach decided to gather together a group of six concertos that had already been written and send them to the Margrave of Brandenburg. He hoped either to be given a job by the nobleman, or maybe to be given cash for his work. As far as the records show, neither of these outcomes actually happened. So, Bach was paid nothing for one of the most amazing sets of concertos ever.

## 68: Why is Rossini's *Rice Aria* so called?

Some composers labour for months over every note of their music and die having produced merely a handful of short masterpieces. Not so with Rossini, who seemed almost to perspire music. The entire overture to *The Barber of Seville* was allegedly finished in just 13 days. When he came to write his 1813 opera *Tancredi*, he allegedly dashed off one aria, "Di tanti palpiti", in just the time it took for his rice to boil. Hence the nickname.

## 69: How did Fauré choose his wife?

This seems one of the more unbelievable answers in this book, but we promise it's true. Fauré allowed a friend to introduce him to three different women. He found all three of them pleasant, but could not decide which to take as his wife. So, he wrote their names out on paper, put them in a hat … and picked one. It was Marie Frémiet, the daughter of a sculptor. He met her and married her. Lucky girl.

## 70: Was Palestrina really called Palestrina?

Well, yes and no. Palestrina is, in fact, the name of a small town just outside Rome. The composer Palestrina's full name, as far as we know today, was Giovanni da Palestrina, which in English, translates as "John from Palestrina". So, all we really know about his name is that he was called John.

## 71: How is a concerto different from a concerto grosso?

A standard concerto today consists of a solo instrumentalist accompanied by an orchestra. Originally, though, the soloist role was taken by a *group* of instrumentalists, playing the virtuoso role, separate from the orchestra. This type of set-up is called a concerto grosso. Gradually, across the years, the number of people in the group has diminished and the single soloist and orchestra format – a solo concerto – has become dominant.

## 72: Was Bach a rambler?

He did like a good long walk, but he was more of a getting-from-A-to-B kind of guy, than someone who liked to admire the scenery. He became famous for walking from Arnstadt to Lübeck, a round trip of some 400 miles, just to hear the organist Buxtehude play. And this wasn't a one-off. Bach would think nothing of walking around 60 miles or so, from Hamburg to Celle, just to hear music.

## 73: Bach and Handel were born in the same year, but did they ever meet?

Not only were they born in the same year, they were both born in Germany and they were the top composers of their generation. Sadly, they never actually clapped eyes on each other though. There was one occasion when it *almost* happened. In the autumn of 1719, Bach travelled to Halle, with the express intention of meeting his rival, but Handel had already left for England.

## 74: Did Grieg write Delius's *On Hearing the First Cuckoo in Spring?*

No, of course he didn't. But it's not such a silly question. Delius did write *On Hearing the First Cuckoo in Spring*, although the central tune is not an original Delius. It is a folksong, which he arranged, embellished and generally improved upon. So where did Delius find the folksong? In Grieg's 1896 book of *19 Norwegian Folk Tunes.* So it would be true to say that Grieg did have an influential part to play in the work.

## 75: Who is the patron saint of music?

St Cecilia. Her original associations with music are a little lost in the mists of time. As early as the fourth century, she was already being linked with music-making. Cecilia herself was the daughter of a Roman senator, who declined to consummate her marriage, as she was betrothed to an angel. The Rome Academy of Music adopted her as their patron saint in 1584 and the connection still exists today.

## 76: What is the strangest piece of classical music ever written?

This very much depends on your definition of strange. Rossini's *Cat Duet,* in which two sopranos miaow at each other for the whole song strikes us as very odd. But, in our opinion, it is John Cage who wrote the strangest work of all. In *0′00″*, the heavily amplified performer feeds vegetables into a blender and then drinks the resulting juice. Imagine how you'd feel if you'd paid money to commission that little gem.

## 77: Was Paganini possessed?

The only thing Paganini was possessed of was a phenomenal violin technique. Beyond that, he was simply a clever marketing man, who thought that a bit of a "diabolical" reputation would persuade people to flock to his concerts. And he was right. Intriguingly, when he was dying, he refused the last rites because he didn't think he was going to die. His optimism was misplaced but his decision meant that the church declined to bury him in consecrated ground. The "devil" myth continued.

## 78: Who was the Elise mentioned in *Für Elise*?

Elise didn't exist. Therese did, though. This is a good lesson to composers, GPs and pharmacists everywhere: ensure that your handwriting is legible. Beethoven dedicated this *Bagatelle* to a girl for whom he had the hots, one Therese Malfatti. When the manuscript was found after her death, Beethoven's publisher misread the scrawly handwriting. There is no truth in the rumour that a similar mistake happened with his *Symphony No 3* and that it was actually written for a girl called Erica.

## 79: Who wrote Gounod's *Ave Maria*?

Gounod did. And so did J S Bach. It started life as a *Prelude in C* by Bach. Over a hundred years later, Gounod decided to add a separate tune over the top, originally for violin. He called it *Meditation on Bach's Prelude for Piano.* Later, the words of the *Ave Maria* were added. Gounod obviously wanted to make sure that he would be credited with the work's paternity, as he intriguingly decided to add one extra bar of music to Bach's original piano part.

## 80: Who wrote *Pictures at an Exhibition?*

The obvious answer is Moussorgsky, but a more correct answer would be Moussorgsky, Rimsky-Korsakov and Ravel. The story goes like this: in 1874, Moussorgsky wrote the piece for piano. When he died, his friend Rimsky-Korsakov tweaked it and generally brushed it up in order to publish it as a piano suite. Then, in 1922, Ravel came along and re-imagined it as an orchestral suite. This final version was used as the theme tune for the television comedy *The New Statesman.*

## 81: Did Tchaikovsky kill himself?

Officially, he died of cholera in 1893, possibly contracted through drinking infected drinking water. Much later, the theory was published that he took his own life in a soldier's honour killing because of a scandal involving his homosexuality. To invoke that old cliché ... in truth, we will never know.

## 82: Was Dvořák really a trainspotter?

Indeed, he was. He ardently kept track of train schedules and was often to be found outside Czech train stations, getting a "spot" on. Some stories have him visiting train drivers and stepping up on the plate. He had a similar passion for ships, loving nothing better than a trip to the harbour while he was working in America. Still, we guess it could have been worse. Oh dear, in fact it was. He was also a pigeon-fancier. Now, don't get us started ...

## 83: Why did Rossini give up composing?

He was one of the most successful composers of his day. Up until the age of 37, he wrote his little hands off, stumping up hit after hit. Then, in 1829, he virtually stopped composing altogether. There have been many theories put forward, but we think that he had made his money and wanted to enjoy himself. He was a real bon-viveur and an amazing cook, who gave us the famous recipe for Tournedos Rossini. He simply wanted to live a little.

## 84: Was Beethoven related to royalty?

Some said Beethoven was the King of Prussia's love child. Others claimed he was the son of Frederick the Great. Beethoven himself did nothing to dissuade those who believed him to come from a noble lineage. The truth was a little more mundane. Bizarrely, his name translates as "Ludwig of the Beetroot Farms". It turns out that his ancestors were in fact Liège bumpkins. But who can blame him for trying it on?

## 85: In Tchaikovsky's ballet *The Nutcracker* there is a *Dance of the Mirlitons*. What is a mirliton?

Without putting to finer point on it, a mirliton is, at its most basic, a kazoo. To be strictly accurate, it is a type of blown instrument which used a skin or membrane within its design. The ballet's original choreographer, Petipa, called for "little flutes made of reed, stopped at either end with gold-beater's skin". Sounds like a posh kazoo to us.

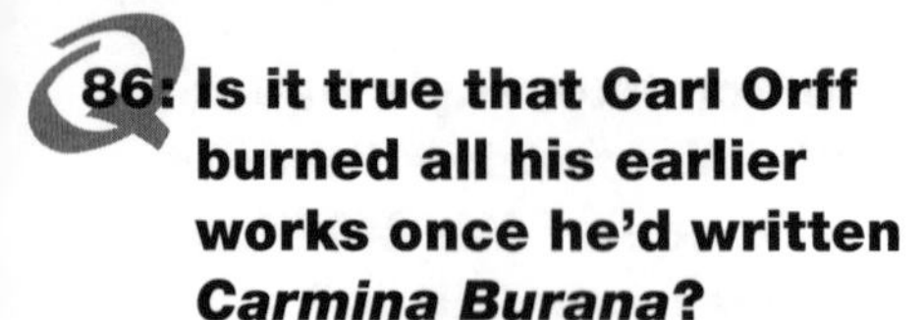

## 86: Is it true that Carl Orff burned all his earlier works once he'd written *Carmina Burana*?

Orff quickly realised that he had a hit on his hands with *Carmina Burana.* He believed that his compositions that followed this work were infinitely superior to the music he wrote beforehand. He is on record as saying, "With *Carmina Burana,* my collected works begin." He even wrote to his publisher, asking that his previous works be destroyed. They weren't.

## 87: What do people mean by "programme music"?

The term "programme music" has nothing to do with the theme tune to *Coronation Street.* Programme music is the stuff which is meant to tell a story or paint a picture when you listen to it. This is the music that is designed by the composer with a narrative in mind. Vivaldi's *Four Seasons* is a good example of programme music, as each separate concerto is created so that it sounds like the corresponding season.

## 88: Why are all musical markings in Italian?

It's hard to pin down the centre of the cultural world today, but when classical music was going through its formative years, there was simply no doubt. It was Italy and so all the instructions were written in Italian. They seem to have an inordinately large number of words for "slow", including *adagio*, *andante*, *andantino*, *largo*, *larghetto* and *lento.* If we don't stop now, we'll never get to the end of the book.

## 89: Was Elgar a "dog person" or a "cat person"?

Without doubt, Sir Edward Elgar was a dog person. He had wanted a dog for most of his life but only took the plunge after the death of his wife, Alice. At that point, he befriended a King Charles spaniel, Marco, and a cairn terrier, Mina. They became his constant companions and he would even set them places at his dinner table. Once, he even signed off a radio broadcast of one of his works with the words, "Goodnight, everybody. Goodnight, Marco."

## 90: Just how *pianissimo* can you get?

Composers write the letter ***p*** on manuscripts to indicate that the musician should play softly. So how far can you go? Well, ***pp*** (short for *pianissimo*) means that you should play very softly and ***ppp*** is fairly common, although it translates as *pianississimo*. Tchaikovsky once wrote a part of his *Pathétique Symphony* as ***ppppp***. In the Italian, this is *pianississississimo*. We're not sure that we'd realise that anyone performing at this volume was still actually playing any notes.

## 91: What is secular music?

This is the umbrella term for all music that is not religious. When the rules of Western music were being laid down, the Church was very much in charge and, as a result, music was generally written in order to praise God. Indeed, the Church even opposed non-vocal music for a time, believing that, without words, there could be no overt praising of God. Secular music eventually gained ground in the Baroque and Classical eras.

## 92: What is a canon?

Nothing to do with guns firing in the *1812 Overture* here. A canon is a type of music that would suit people who like Sudoku. It all centres on the shape of a tune being reflected again and again throughout a piece. The best known canon in classical music is by Pachelbel. However, you might well know a canon better as being a *round* from your years in the playground. Think *London's Burning* or *Frère Jacques* and you've got the idea.

## 93: What was the most important year in classical music?

The answer to this question is always going to be subjective, but we reckon that it would be hard to beat 1685, the year when both George Frideric Handel and Johann Sebastian Bach were both born. There isn't another year when two such great composers took their first breaths. Evidently, middle names which you used throughout your life were also obviously very much in vogue that year.

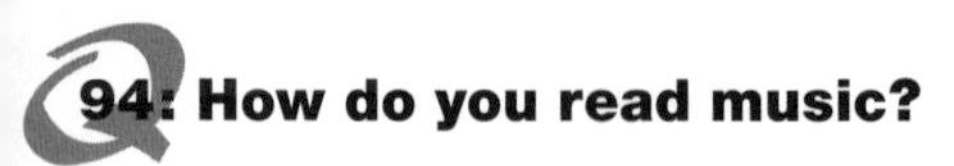

# 94: How do you read music?

Although a music score can appear to be a daunting wall of black and white hieroglyphs, it is, in fact, disarmingly simple to read music. It's a bit like a graph in maths. The higher up the lines you go – just as in the *y* axis in maths – the higher up the pitch of the music goes. The further *along* the lines the note goes – just as in the *x* axis – the longer it lasts. It all starts as simply as that.

Going deeper, the top set of five lines, known as the treble stave, is for the higher notes. The bottom set, called the bass stave, is for the lower ones.

A key signature, using ♯ and ♭ symbols to indicate *sharp* or *flat,* tells the player which set of notes to use and a couple of numbers tell them how many beats to count in each section. Beyond this, there are just a bunch of rules to master. If you can learn to read a map, then you can learn to read a piece of music.

## 95: Why is Tchaikovsky's *Symphony No 6* described as being "pathetic"?

The dictionary definition of "pathetic" is "causing or evoking pity, sympathy or sadness". Given that Tchaikovsky died just nine days after his *Symphony No 6 "The Pathétique"* was premiered, it seems a good title. And yet, Tchaikovsky hated it and he begged his publishers to remove the subtitle, which incidentally translates more as "passionate" or "emotional" in the native Russian. The title stuck though, outlasting Tchaikovsky by a good century or so.

## 96: What is the most unusual title for a classical work?

There's no doubt whatsoever in our minds who walks off with the award for the weirdest collection of titles in the repertoire. Erik Satie may be most famous for his *Gymnopédies,* but he also wrote works called *Veritable Flabby Preludes (for a Dog)*; *Sketches and Exasperations of a Big Boob Made of Wood*; *Five Grins or Mona Lisa's Moustache*; *Waltz of the Chocolate Almonds* and *Things Seen from the Right and Left without Spectacles.* Brilliantly barking mad!

## 97: Who would be regarded as the ultimate "composer's composer"?

A difficult one to measure, but if we're looking at a league table of which great composer the other great composers have sampled in their music, then Paganini must rank near the top. Variations on his *Caprice No 24* have been written by a host of luminaries including Franz Liszt, Johannes Brahms, Sergei Rachmaninoff, Witold Lutosławski and Andrew Lloyd Webber. Even the great jazz clarinettist Benny Goodman penned a version.

## 98: Why do people shout "Bravo" at the end of an opera or concert?

The word is Italian and originally meant "wild" or "excellent". Less common these days, it can often be found uttered by more experienced music-goers, some of whom still remember Guido d'Arezzo inventing the stave. Strictly speaking, *bravo* should only be used when cheering a solo male artist, and *brava* when cheering a solo female artist. Pedantically speaking, when cheering a group (mixed or otherwise) you should yell *"Bravi!"* And then hide.

## 99: What is the weirdest instrument in music?

Several contenders here. The Sousaphone (named after the American composer) is a little odd. You have to wrap it around your body and end up looking like an oversized gramophone player. Leaving aside the Pikasso guitar (amazing) and the Sea Organ (strange), our vote for the weirdest of the lot goes to the Theremin, invented by Léon Theremin in 1919. It consists of two metal antennae, which sense the motion of the player's hands – so you never actually touch it.

## 100: Does listening to classical music make you more intelligent?

Some scientific experiments have suggested that listening to Mozart's music can improve an individual's spatial-temporal reasoning. This is known as the "Mozart Effect". Whether it's true or not, there is no scientific research to suggest that classical music has a detrimental effect to our wellbeing and as it's completely calorie- and fat-free, we're all for it.

## 101: Is classical music dead?

Absolutely not! Classical music is alive and thriving. There is a huge amount of it being written today. The Welsh composer Karl Jenkins is consistently the highest-placed living composer in the Classic FM Hall of Fame, our annual barometer of classical music tastes. Aside from film soundtrack writers, other popular living composers among our listeners include John Rutter, Philip Glass, John Tavener, Michael Nyman, Arvo Pärt, Henryk Górecki and Peter Maxwell Davies. Check them out!